MALE BAGGAGE

Quinton Morgan

Printed in the United States of America

Create Space, 2014

ISBN-13: 9780692336373
ISBN-10: 0692336370

Create Space Publishing
www.createspace.com

Chief and Editor of Strut! The Magazine

"*MALE BAGGAGE is a clever read about issues that (if not properly addressed) have the potential to disturb, disrupt and destroy the best of relationships. Every Guy will read the descriptions and wonder IS THIS ME? And Every Female will ask DO I KNOW HIM? Once we swallow the pill, accept the truth and see the reality, we can move forward with the healing... Individual Healing and then the Healing of Our Relationships. While the surface focus highlights the flaws of some men, when truly analyzed, we see how some women add to this baggage. This book will definitely serve as an icebreaker and provide the platform for conversations that catapult awareness and change.*"

~Dr. Darcova Triplett~

Acknowledgements

I wrote this book to address the rampant epidemic of Male Baggage. While our society has varied and diverse correlations to the expression 'Male Baggage,' let's agree that its general concern is with unresolved issues of an emotional nature. Oftentimes, this emotional baggage proves to be detrimental to any relationship. Visually speaking, male baggage looks like a man carrying all the disappointments, wrongs and trauma of the past, thus creating a heavy load on the mind, body, and spirit. The purpose of this book is to expose the delusional forms of how this damaging baggage appears in relationships. A few forms of male baggage that I will discuss between these sheets are Scum Bag, Baby Bag, Tote Bag, Paper Bag, Overnight Bag, Nickel Bag, Punching bag. These forms carry a negative connotation and are simply created by *life experiences*. By analyzing this recurring theme in past relationships, we become better prepared to leave the bags at the door so that present relationships have the opportunity to prosper.

Table of Contents

Chapter 1. The Scum Bag/Player

To understand the inner thinking of a Scum Bag, we must first understand the definition of scum. Thorndike Barnhart defines scum as a foul extraneous matter that forms on the surface of certain materials. It can also be described as a low, worthless, or evil person. Scum Bag according to Quinton references the player because he is the lowest of the low. Only dirt, the soil of the earth, is as low as scum.

The Scum Bag is a player and the player is a low life who does not deserve the time of day from any decent, determined, deserving woman. Screwing around is just one of the many disgusting things he does. Scum Bags really love playing games on women. He is the type of guy who loves to send mixed signals and play with a woman's emotions in the process.

The Scum Bag plays the games for so many reasons. He plays games just to test the woman. He wants to test her love, loyalty and emotional capability. He also does this to test her level of understanding as well as her intelligence and the way she reasons. Some play it when they really want to obtain something from the woman and they know that the only way to make her reconsider is to insert the Shock Effect which is warranted by toying with her emotions.

The Scum Bag recognizes that some women can be emotionally damaged and they use this female shortcoming to their advantage. The Scum Bag's angle is to lead a woman with false promises. It is to deceivingly promise commitment and future benefits in order to mislead her into giving her very all. In return, he gives very little. A player will get the attention of several women and trick one of them into giving him what he wants for his own selfish purposes.

The Scum Bag sets out to see how far he can get with game. Once he realizes that he can game you and not get caught, the entire situation becomes a battlefield of physiological warfare. The Scum Bag only thinks of himself and is only committed to playing games with your mind. Although never stated directly, the Scum Bag has no intention of settling down. This is never blatantly communicated because the result will not be another victim. The Scum Bag sees dating and sex as sport. He gets a rush out of meeting a new woman and adding her to his extensive list of women. In all actuality, he gets a kick out of this behavior. To him it is fun to be with different women because at his core, he feels that's the nature of the being. The Scum Bag thrives on a plethora of women. This man is never happy with one woman and he always seeks sex outside the relationship. He is always in need of a little side action. His strategy is to say I love you, play house and then get sex. When the sex dies down, he repeats the cycle with the next woman.

Why does the Scum Bag act this way? According to Kat Hertlein, Ph.D., professor of human development at the University of Nevada - Las Vegas and a marriage and family therapist, approximately 40% of men seek sexual satisfaction outside their relationships. That estimate was consistent with results from the famous Kinsey sex study which reported that 50% of U.S. men cheat at some point in their relationships. David Buss, professor of psychology at the University of Texas and author of The Evolution of Desire: Strategies of Human Mating asserts that the leading cause for the Scum Bag's behavior is: Some men crave sexual "variety." Professor Buss goes on to state that "They've evolved the desire to be with different women."

Simple biology also plays a key role. It is very simple for men to reproduce (one act of sex versus nine months of pregnancy for women), so to create as many offspring as possible, the Scum Bag is biologically programmed to mate with many women. Another significant factor is the thrill. These guys who engage in such affairs are getting in touch with their inner caveman: It the danger of playing with fire that adds to the level of excitement.

Whether it's evolution, biology or simple novelty, infidelity researchers agree that some men do seek different sex partners. Nonetheless, the decision to cheat or to be a Scum Bag is entirely in a man's control. "Most men don't act

on those desires because they don't want to jeopardize social reputations or relationships," says University of Texas' Buss.

Chapter 2. Baby Bag/Baby Mamma Drama

What is a baby Mamma? Society defines her as a woman who shares a child with a man whom she is no longer in a relationship with. Additional dynamics include the element that she causes problems within future relationships because he is still sleeping with her. Take note of the interesting situations created by and perpetrated by this man. The dramatic climax builds from him still sleeping with her and refusing to put her in her place because if he does she may tell all of their secrets.

This is one type of man that can really try your nerves. I say that because he will come off as a great Dad to his children but he is only going over to the children's Mother's house to have sex (this you will never know.) Then he comes back in your face, has sex with you, kisses you, and talks to you as if he has done nothing wrong. This is the type of guy who actually doesn't mention much about his baby Mamma. If he does, he acts as though he can't stand her. In reality, he still tells her that he loves her behind closed doors. When you ask him about her, he just blows it off as if she is nothing. Here is the thing, you have to really watch it if he makes this statement "I will always love her because she is the mother of my child." This is just like saying, "I will always love the person that took my virginity because he/she was the first one to have sex with me."

In some cases, the baby Mamma will constantly call your phone (restricted) just to cause problems within your relationship. Once you communicate this with him he asks you," Why would it be her?" He responds in this way just to throw you off even further from his cheating ways. This guy will never respond back to a text or a call when he goes to see his baby Mamma. The reason he doesn't respond is because if he does the baby Mamma will get upset and blow his cover. He sometimes will not even tell you that he has even seen his child. The only way you find out is because you see pictures on Facebook or some other form of Social Media. He will include you with his future goals and will tell you that he wants to marry you. This is a smoke screen only to keep you at bay so that he can continue to screw his baby Mamma right up under your nose without you finding out.

The Baby Bag always communicates with his baby's Mamma in an unhealthy way. He will always use the phrase, "She is crazy." But watch how he reacts to her so called craziness. If he is calling her crazy and she is the Mother of his child, can you imagine what he is saying about you to her? And this is what keeps the drama going. He is actually keeping the baby Momma on a string by sexing her and talking about you to her. This gives her hope that someday he will leave you and return to her.

Sometimes the drama is actually a cover-up for how he really feels. He may still have feelings for her; in fact, he probably does. Instead of accepting the fact that love still exists in his heart, he may not be mature enough to accept it for what it is so he continues to string both of you along. He may not realize that the love he feels doesn't have to expressed in a sexual way. Or she doesn't want him to believe he still loves her so he acts out in ways that supposedly express hatred or discontent when, really, it's all a cover-up for his true feelings.

The Baby Bag will bring this baby Mamma baggage by allowing his baby Mamma to talk crazy to you. She will sometimes claim that she is still with this man. He will explain this action by saying, "she's just lying" and "she said all of those things to you out of her frustration because she still wants me." Fact is, she does want him BECAUSE he is still sleeping with her. The baby Momma will always give you little hints that they are still sleeping together and he will always blow it off. This guy is an absolute mess.

Here are a couple of pockets in that Baby Bag. He will leave you at his family's cookout with the explanation that he is going to get his child so that his child can be a part of the festivities. He will be gone for hours. He does this to make sure you stay in place so that he can do his dirt without getting caught by you. This also is done so that he can screw his baby's Momma really quick before he brings his child over to the cookout. Another pocket in that Baby Bag is child support. The baby Bag and the baby Mamma will often be mad at each other then she will threaten him with child support. All of a sudden, they will be like best friends and he will start telling her about your situation; talking about you like a dog. This will give her leverage against you but he doesn't care since he knows all he has to do is tell you that she is lying… and you will believe him.

You really want to know something that's messed up in this type of situation? What else is messed up is his family will keep inviting the baby Mamma over to the cookouts as if she is part of the family and he will say nothing about it. She accepts the invites just to let you know that she is still relevant in his life. Most of the time she doesn't have a life a life of her own. Her life revolves around trying to make his life and your life miserable.

Chapter 3. Tote Bag/ The Unemployed Man

To understand this type of man you must first know the definition of a tote bag. We know that a tote bag is simply a large bag used for carrying a number of items. This is the perfect definition for this type of man because you will be toting his butt around along with a number of his self-imposed issues. The Tote bag is very comfortable with you taking care of him and regardless of how much you complain, he refuses to get a job. He actually feels no kinda way about having a girlfriend or wife take complete care of him.

Even though you did not set out to support this type of man, it just somehow sneaks up on you. It all starts with "loaning" this man a few dollars that he never pays it back. In some cases, when couples are dating, the woman will want to prove that she will support her man through anything and any situation. She will make sure that she helps him as much as possible, and in doing this she believes that the man will respect her for this. Unfortunately, what happens is the exact opposite.

The Tote bag comes off as the love of your life. Sometimes the woman will be so taken by this guy that she will nonchalantly pay for their dates. Once this is done it is game time. He has all the qualities you look for in a man and potential husband. You completely submit yourself to him. You often prepare meals for him at your house and he happily wolfs them down. After that, he will start calling for dinner daily. As he eats your food, he will charm you with jokes and tell you how great of a cook you are. Before you know it you are providing him with lavish gifts, buying clothes, and giving him pocket money. You may even cosign for a car for him just so he can get around since he is in-between jobs and supposedly looking for work. He hardly contributes much towards anything you all may do. This guy will move in with you with the promises of marrying you because he knows this is the only way he can keep you on his string. He always has an excuse on why he can't help on the bills. As a matter of a fact he will be saving the money that you give him so that he can use that money to take out another woman. This man will use you until you actually cut him off.

The thing about The Tote Bag Man is that he is just lazy. He will use your money to flaunt in front of other women as if it is his and he will talk about you behind your back to the other woman as if you are the problem within the relationship. He will take your car and drop you off at work while he goes out to flex in your ride while he is supposed to be looking for a job. He will go as far as to dress the part as if he is going on job interviews but actually will be taking other women out in your car with your money. You will be just lugging his butt around and the entire time and he will be bringing you down financially, emotionally, and spiritually.

Chapter 4. Paper Bag/The Alcoholic

The Alcoholic is a person that has problems controlling his drinking, being preoccupied with alcohol, and will continue to use alcohol even when it causes problems. The Paper Bag Man will develop a physical dependence for alcohol, and you will never be able to predict how much he will drink, how long he will drink, and he doesn't seem to care about the consequences that will occur because of his drinking.

With The paper bag Man, it typically starts when he comes home from work. If there's a party or an event on the weekend, he may drink more. This pattern can, and often does, go on for many months or even years. Gradually the atmosphere in the home begins to change. The conversations seem to slow down, the interactions begin to center around what needs to get done rather than how each person's day was, and the energy in the house becomes more tense. Sometimes this guy becomes short, impatient and irritating to be around. Once this occurs you will become more distant from him.

The Paper Bag Man will always be in denial of his alcohol abuse. He will also refuse to accept that he has a problem. There are several signs that point to relationship turmoil as a result of this alcohol problem that will require professional help. As the relationship continues you all will tend to argue and fight over the use or purchase of alcohol. You will find yourself having to cover or make excuses for this type of guy due to excessive alcohol use on why he may not be able to show up to social events or family gatherings. You will find that your time together will be centered on drinking. The Paper Bag will show affection only when under the influence and he may also become aggressive during the sexual activity.

The alcoholic disorder can affect a couple because alcohol is often used to self-medicate and numb feelings that the drinker is unable to cope with, according to many doctors. They also note that alcohol may provide a calming effect at first by allowing alcoholics to escape their problems, but with continued use, as the alcohol wears off, they are often more anxious and may fall into depression or have sleep difficulties. Emotional and physical pain alerts people that something in the mind or body needs to be attended to. When alcohol abusers numb out these signals on a consistent basis, emotional connectivity with their partners may be lost in the process.

When this man, the alcoholic, comes home, he may sometimes verbally abuse you when he is drunk. He may even physically abuse you as well when he is under the influence. The Paper Bag Man may sometimes go on binges when he doesn't return home for a few days after he has drank up his entire paycheck from work. The alcoholic can be the nicest guy in the world until he starts drinking.

The scary thing about this man is that he can sometimes turn this abuse towards the kids. This type of abuse can make the kids scared of him, make them fear for your safety, and has the potential to cause long term mental damage to yourself along with your children. This type of damage can cause you to go into a depression and sometimes it may even cause you to start demonstrating this same type of behavior. This in turn can cause more emotional damage to your children. He may even physically abuse your kids as well when he is under the influence of alcohol. With this happening you can find yourself in double trouble. Now you not only have to worry your safety but you also have to worry about the safety of your children.

Chapter 5. The Overnight Bag/ Hit It and Quit It

To understand the Overnight Bag Man you must understand what an overnight bag actually is. An overnight bag is a small piece of luggage used to carry items needed for an overnight stay. This term or phrase is very appropriate for this type of man. He basically comes over just for sex and nothing else and leaves early in the morning before anyone can spot him over to your place of residence.

This type of man doesn't want to commit to a healthy relationship. He only wants to satisfy his own selfish sexual needs. He doesn't even care if you cum or not during the sexual act. He just wants to achieve an orgasm then leave. He doesn't care about your kids, your wellbeing, or even just your life in general. He just wants you for sex and that is it. If you ask him about commitment he will avoid the conversation or change the subject without you even understanding what just happened.

What you must understand about the Overnight Bag Man is that he doesn't want to be with you. He doesn't want to take you out in public or really converse with you unless it is about sex. You may play the period game with him. The period game is when you get him to come over with an intense sex conversation but once he gets there and tries to get a little, you tell him that you are on your period. When you play this game he will find an excuse to leave all of a sudden. Normally, he would at least stay until the wee hours in the morning, but once you mention your period, he is gone within about 10- 20 minutes of that comment.

The Overnight Bag Man will actually be a great lover. This is how he is able to keep you on the hook for so long. The sex is amazing and he will blow your mind sexually. The things he do to you in bed have never been done before and if so it wasn't done to the level that he is actually doing them. The Overnight Bag Man will tell you everything that you want to hear but never follow up on his promises. He will tell you that he is going to take you out one day but never does. He will tell you that he will help you when you are down but never will. He will always have an excuse on why he can't take you out or be seen in public with you. The bottom line is you are blinded by the sex. You actually have thoughts of being in a relationship with this type of guy. But you are quickly reminded that he is not for you because of his continuous unaccommodating behavior.

You know what is the kicker about The Overnight Bag Man? The fact that you will actually do for him all the type of things you would do for a boyfriend. You will cook for him, run his bath water, and make sure he is completely taken care of while he is in your presence. He repays you by leaving you in the wee hours of the morning with nothing but a wet rear end and empty dreams. Hit it and quit it, this is what this man does and will continue to do until he gets tired of playing these games and becomes a real man.

Chapter 6. Nickel Bag/The Hustler

The hustler is a person who employs fraudulent or unscrupulous methods to obtain money; swindler. The Nickel Bag Man can sometimes be described as a drug dealer. A hustler never really has a job or a steady stream of income. But he will always have money. One thing about the hustler, he will hustle you into thinking he is a great guy but he really is not. He will always put your family and your life in jeopardy with his illegal ways of living.

Another thing about this type of man is that he will never file taxes and is more than likely behind in child support. This is a trip because though he is making money under the table, he doesn't use it for any good. He will actually ask you for your tax money. Around tax time he will start being really nice to you. Treating you like a queen, and saying all the right things. This is a tactic used to get in good with you so that he can get the bulk of your tax money. You will give him the money with hopes of a promising future, besides he is your man and you support your man right? He knows you are weak for him and he uses his hustler mentality to pimp you out of your cash.

Something else about this guy is that you may never really be able to keep a tab on him. It raises the question though, as to what really concerns you? He makes you unhappy with his inability to provide for you financially on a consistent basis. Or are you uncomfortable with the fact that he is outside of the socio economic status of the men you would rather date? You have a steady job that pays fairly well and when your man is reaping his occasional windfall, you benefit, to a certain degree. Due to the nature of his hustling, his income is so unpredictable. Can you appreciate and accept his way of life and work with him despite the apparent financial shortcomings? If you decide to CONTINUE in the relationship, it can't be because you feel as though you can't do any better or out of pity. It must be that you care for this person and want to share your life with him. It is senseless, however, to remain in the relationship and be unhappy.

You should be concerned about dating someone who is involved with this type of lifestyle. Do not be fooled by The Overnight Man. He may be making a lot of money at times. Be wary though that life may not be necessarily better in the higher socio-economic bracket, as financial stability does not always equate to emotional and psychological stability.

Chapter 7. The Punching Bag/ The Abuser

I saved this type of guy for the last chapter because this is one of the most serious types of situations that you may find yourself involved in. Also due to the most resent circumstances surrounding our professional athletes, this has brought this type of guy to the forefront of social media, internet blogs, and the topic of various television programs. To recognize The Punching Bag Man, you have to understand what the meaning of physical abuse actually is. Physical abuse is an act of another party involving contact intended to cause feelings of physical pain, injury, or other physical suffering or bodily harm.

BatteredWomen.com indicates there are warning signs individuals should be aware of when it comes to a potentially abusive situation. Here are a few:

Want instant gratification.

Have an insatiable ego.

Have low self-esteem.

Make frequent promises to improve.

Perceives themselves as socially inadequate.

Becomes jealous easily.

Isolates significant others from friends and family.

Ignores or lacks awareness of personal boundaries.

Believes forcible behavior is acceptable if it's for the greater good.

Feels no guilt after explosive episodes.

Demanding and assaultive during sexual activities.

Uses "playful" force during sex.

Uses threats to control another individual.

Can switch between abuse forms depending on which tactics are most effective.

Blames others for the abuse when it happens.

Objectifies women.

Maintains tight control over finances.

Uses children as means of manipulation.

Makes you appear "crazy;" demeaning toward you in front of others.

Makes a joke out of the violent situation.

Quick to become involved in relationships.

They can be alcohol or drug users.

His background may explain why he abuses you. While it is important to realize that not all abusers were abused as children, and that many if not most people who are abused do not go on to become abusers themselves, child abuse is most likely the single largest risk factor – biological, psychological, or sociocultural – for later adult abusive behavior, according to" David M. Allen, M.D., Professor of Psychiatry Emeritus, University of Tennessee Health Science Center. Dr. Allen explains significant family dysfunction of one sort or another is almost always present in the backgrounds of repetitive abusers. These dysfunctional patterns often do not stop when abused children grow up, but continue in modified form as long as the involved parents are still living.

Most abusers have what is called a "narcissistic personality disorder." Those with "narcissistic" traits often feel duty bound to be in charge and take care of others while simultaneously being starved for admiration. Those with "borderline" traits can be help-rejecting complainers who usually seem both miserable and unappreciative. While the male is typically the one who becomes violent, this is not always the case. Like many bullies, an abuser uses physical threats or actions when feeling impotent, frustrated," says Herold J. Kreisman, M.D., co-author of I Hate You, Don't Leave Me: Understanding the Borderline Personality, and, Sometimes I Act Crazy: Living with Borderline Personality Disorder. "Borderline personality traits may be characterized by explosive impulsivity and extreme mood changes that change from loving feelings to hateful feelings when frustrated or angry.

When dealing with an abusive man you may suffer from post-traumatic stress syndrome, one symptom of which is dissociation, which often creates such profound detachment from the reality of the abuse that sufferers scarcely remember being hurt at all. According to Dr. Craig Malkin, phycologist and instructor at Harvard Medical School. Dissociating victims can't leave the abuse because they aren't psychologically present enough to recall the pain of what happened.

You may be afraid to leave this type of man. And who really can blame you based upon number of well-documented hurdles to victims leaving their abusive partner. Sometimes you may be cut off from friends and financial supports. Also, more than 70 percent of domestic violence injuries and murders happen after the victim has left. So I can understand if it may feel safer to stay. But perhaps one of the most formidable and dangerous obstacles you may face is your own guilt and shame; you have become incredibly adept at blaming yourself for the abuse.

Chapter 8. Possible Solutions

This is what I think you must do to avoid dating the Scum Bag/ Player. You need to SLOW down anyone who is looking to move quickly. Players are interested in getting what they want as quickly as possible. You must lay some ground rules for yourself establishing time limitations for different stages of your relationship. When you do this, you will be able to recognize a player, as they will become anxious and impatient according to Ehow internet source.

Watch out for men that are more focused on how they look (i.e. stuck on themselves). A player is good looking and knows it. They tend to think they are entitled to treat others poorly because of this "fact." They may also think that they are God's gift to women.

When and if you are dating the Scum bag/Player you should dump him quick and not allow him to treat you any kind of way. Let him know that you are the prize, let him know that he is lucky to have you. Hell, because you have to think, he is the one that chose to talk to you. I'm not saying you should be arrogant or smug but just let him know that you are not going to accept that player type of behavior and that you deserve better than the way he is treating you and there will not be any second chances to screw you over. Communicate these things to him in the very beginning so that he will understand when and if he goes outside of the lines or boundaries that you have placed that you will leave and not put up with that foolishness. Dealing with baby Momma drama can be very difficult. But dealing with a man who continues to sleep with the Mother of his child can be even more difficult. If your man is still dealing with the mother of his child in an inappropriate way the best way to deal with him is to first confront him with the issues that you may have with him. Do not confront the Mother of the child. Your problem is with him not her. You have to set boundaries and let him know what you will and will not put up with. You cannot allow him to get away with sleeping with her. Once you get wind of his infidelity concerning you should get the hell on. The problem is, if you take him back you will feel as though you will not be able to trust him with the Mother of his child anytime that they are alone or anytime that he goes over to pick up his child. You will always think they are sexing behind your back. So the best thing to do is to kick him to the curb. Do not allow him to just continue to disrespect you.

In order to deal with the Tote Bag, the unemployed man, you must possess an incredible amount of patience. If the unemployed man is really trying then you should stick by him and help him through this low point in his life. He will appreciate it. On the other hand, if he is using you, lying to you, and allowing you to take care of him then you have to kick him to the curb. Well, not right off the bat. But you have to let him know that you will not deal with a man that doesn't work. Even the Bible says that a man that doesn't work should not eat. So just that alone tells you what you need to do in this situation. No man likes to feel uncomfortable, so you have to make the situation with him not working uncomfortable as possible. This only applies to the man that is trying to use you to get ahead and not work towards the building up of the relationship. When you get home you must ask him, "Why are you not working?" If he asks you for money you must say, "NO." To keep yourself from even allowing this type of man into your life you must not allow him into your space at first signs of broke!!!!!!!! Sign one: if he says," can I borrow some money I'm a little short, I will pay you back later?" Sign two; if he if he says," Can you get it this time I will pay the next time?" Sign three; "can I borrow your car, mine is not working right now?" Sign four; "can I borrow a few dollars I will pay you back once I GET MY INCOME TAX?" Recognize these few signs and take heed to them. If you address these signs in the beginning you will save yourself many problems and headaches in the end.

The Paper Bag/ alcoholic man is a very touchy and delicate situation to be involved in. You must approach this scenario with purpose, love, and care. According to, About Health internet source, you should not take the alcoholics drinking personally. When alcoholic's promise they will never drink again, but a shortly after making the promise they are back to drinking as much as before it is easy for you to take the broken promises and lies personally. You may tend to think, "If they really love me, they wouldn't lie to me." But if they have become truly ADDICTED TO ALCOHOL, their brain chemistry may have changed to the point that they are completely surprised by some of the choices they make. They may not be in control of their own decision making. Many if you are involved with an alcoholic naturally you will try everything you can think of to get the man to stop drinking. Unfortunately, this usually results in leaving you feeling lonely and frustrated. You may tell yourself that surely there is something that you can do, but the reality is not even alcoholics can control their drinking, try as they may. Make no mistake about it;

alcoholism, or alcohol dependence, is a primary, chronic and progressive disease that can be detrimental to your relationship. Out of all the people you could have fallen in love with you just happen to love someone who is probably going to need professional treatment to get healthy again. You can't cure the disease it is up to him to want to stop the abuse. If he says, "I don't have a problem, so don't tell anyone, "usually is the problem in itself. The alcoholic typically does not want anyone to know the level of their alcohol consumption because if someone found out the full extent of the problem, they might try to help or actually insist that you exit the situation if fear for your safety. You should never try to "help" the alcoholic by covering up for their drinking and making excuses for them, If you do this you are playing right into the alcoholic's denial game. Dealing with the problem openly and honestly is the best approach. One problem in dealing with an alcoholic is that what might seem like a reasonable expectation in some circumstances, might be totally unreasonable with an addict. When alcoholics swear to you and to themselves that they will never touch another drop, you might naturally expect that they are sincere and they won't drink again. But with alcoholics, that expectation turns out to be unreasonable. Is it reasonable to expect that he would be honest with you when he is incapable of even being honest with himself? Sometimes while trying to help will actually do something that enables alcoholics to continue along their destructive paths. Find out what enabling is and make sure that you are not doing anything that supports the alcoholic's denial or prevents them from facing the natural consequences of their actions. Most of the time the alcoholic has finally reached out for help when they realized their enabling system was no longer in place. You must make sure that you stay to the course of his awareness and recognition of the problem to insure a healthy relationship for the future.

The Overnight Bag/ hit it and quit it type of man is a man that many women have come across. One of the keys to avoiding this type of man is to not have sex too fast in the first place. Another of many ways is to recognize the signs in the beginning that he is not for you. If a man seems to always be MIA during the weekends, this is a clear sign that he is reserving weekends for someone else on his literal to-do list, or keeping his options open to meet other women. When a girl is just a girl that he just wants for sex, he will never ask her out on a weekend. Weekends are strictly reserved for possible wifey type of women and new possible victims. A guy who is really into you will communicate with you on the regular.

A guy who is in it just for sex, calls, texts, emails, and pops-over only when he is feeling horny and knows that you will indulge his sexual desires. If you are surprised whenever he calls, the chances are, this is a sex only situation. Your dates are always cozy nights in at your crib. Why? Because that is the easiest place to have sex. Avoid him if he spends just enough time together for a little foreplay, sex and maybe a nap. Unless there's time and desire for a round two, a sex-only motivated man will bolt like a thief in the night before you even have time to turn over on his side. Don't even allow him to spend the night unless he is actually your man and you all have established a relationship with boundaries. A secure relationship has great communication. If your communication is only one-sided watch out!!!! The sex-only guy is remorseless when it comes to responding to your texts hours later, days later, or even not at all. When the immediate response is simply to RSVP for sex, consider that. Same goes for phone calls, emails, Facebook messages, tweets or any other form of communication. Here is the situation concerning The Overnight Bag Man, the two of you speak one language: Sex. That's it. If you think hard about it, you may know everything about how he likes "it" but you have no clue where his parents live, what he wanted to be when he grew up, the food that he likes but you do know how he likes it in bed. You should be able to get his attention by your spiritual and mental connection. Those are the type of women that most men will consider as relationship worthy. You don't have to play like a virgin; you just need to offer more than just sex. Watch it if a guy tells you straight up that he doesn't want a girlfriend, doesn't have time for a girlfriend, can't deal with a girlfriend... and just wants to somewhat chill. It is up to you if you want to listen but remember, most guys don't want to deliver news that women don't want to hear unless they really mean it. Know who you are and be in charge of what you want from the beginning. If you leave it up to him, then he probably is going to go for what is easiest and that's never a real true relationship.

When you are involved with the Nickel Bag/hustler type of man please understand that in this situation you already know from the beginning how this relationship is really going to go. You must tell him about your expectations. If you are in a relationship with a hustler, let him know what you want out of him. If he is fearful of getting too close, and you want to take your relationship with him to another level, the two of you are on a different page. Indicate to him what you want out of the relationship, whether it's total commitment, moving in together, or marriage. Ask him if he sees the same for your future together as a couple. The hustler is just that- a hustler, so he has the gift of gab. You have to use logic when you speak. When you are talking to a hustler, it is vital to talk to him in a manner that he can comprehend. To express yourself to a drug dealer, realize that he might not think in "feelings" in the same way that you do. If you utilize logic, he may find talking and opening up to you more comfortable. You may have to distance yourself if necessary. You may need to establish some distance (even if it's just temporary) between yourself and the hustler if he does not take heed to your demands. If you get the impression that he cannot offer you what it is that you want, or even if he straight-out told you that, spend some time apart. He will attempt to reestablish a connection with you if he is ready to open himself up to you. In the meanwhile, you need to move on because if someone isn't ready or willing, you cannot wait around forever. For the most part do not allow him to hustle you. You deserve better than that and know that you are more than that.

The Punching Bag/ abuser is one of the worst types of men that you could ever be involved with. Not because he can possibly possess all the qualities of all the men that I have addressed in the body of the book but because if he doesn't get help he can cause lifelong physiological and emotional damage that can affect everyone in the family forever. I will never advise anyone to ever stay in an abusive relationship. If you are in this type of relationship you must leave. According to ,Wiki How internet source, breaking up may be settled after you've contacted Domestic Violence networks and the police and it's recommended that the best way to break up with a physical or emotional abuser is to keep it as simple as possible. Severe all contact immediately. Clearly say, "This relationship is over and I'm contacting the police if you try to get in touch."

If you feel you must break up with an abusive lover face to face, do it in public, with other people present, and keep the conversation brief. Once you've made the decision to break up, don't try to enter into a negotiation or a discussion with your abuser.

If you live with the Punching Bag Man, it's important to just leave, and then break up in public. Pack an overnight bag and hide it, then when you're ready to leave, just get out as quickly as possible. Only go back to your living space with a few people for support.

Here a few characteristics of an abuser according to Dr. Sam Vaknin: Does he act in a patronizing and condescending manner and criticize you often? Does he emphasize your minutest faults (devalues you) even as he exaggerates your talents, traits, and skills (idealizes you)? Does he call you names, harass, or ridicule you? Is he wildly unrealistic in his expectations from you, from himself, from the budding relationship, and from life in general? Does he respect your boundaries and privacy? Does he ignore your wishes? Does he disrespect your boundaries and treat you as an object or an instrument of gratification? Does he go through your personal belongings while waiting for you to get ready? Does he text or phone you multiple times and incessantly? Does he insist to know where you are or where you have been at all times? Does he go through your Facebook account and question you about your male friends or even female friends? If he is doing the things that I stated he has the chance of being an abuser. I think you should not even give this guy the time of day because if you do this could be the worst mistake of your life… if he doesn't take your life first.

Disclaimer

I, the author of the content in Male Baggage, can assure you, the reader, that any of the opinions expressed here are my own and are a result of the way in which my mind interprets a particular situation and/or concepts. I would like to expressly convey to you if I accidentally defame, purge, humiliate and or hurt someone's person or feelings as a result of reading and/or acting upon any or all of the information and or advice found here in this book, it is entirely unintentional.

Selected Biography and References

This are the references and sources as to where I retrieved some of the information provided within this book.

Thorndike Barnhart defines scum as a foul extraneous matter that forms on the surface of certain materials. Kat Hertlein, Ph.D., professor of human development at the University of Nevada - Las Vegas and a marriage and family therapist, states; approximately 40% of men seek sexual satisfaction outside their relationships. Kinsey sex study which reported that 50% of U.S. men cheat at some point in their relationships. David Buss, professor of psychology at the University of Texas and author of The Evolution of Desire, Strategies of Human Mating asserts that the leading cause for the Scum Bag's behavior is. BatteredWomen.com indicates there are warning signs individuals should be aware of when it comes to a potentially abusive situation. Wiki How internet source, breaking up may be settled after you've contacted Domestic Violence networks" David M. Allen, M.D., Professor of Psychiatry Emeritus, University of Tennessee

Health Science Center. Dr. Allen explains significant family dysfunction of one sort or another is almost always present in the backgrounds of repetitive abusers." David M. Allen, M.D., Professor of Psychiatry Emeritus, University of Tennessee Health Science Center. Dr. Allen explains significant family dysfunction of one sort or another is almost always present in the backgrounds of repetitive abusers. When you do this, you will be able to recognize a player, as they will become anxious and impatient according to Ehow internet source. Dr. Craig Malkin, phycologist and instructor at Harvard Medical School says, "Dissociating victims can't leave the abuse because they aren't psychologically present enough to recall the pain of what happened." The Characteristics of an abuser according to Dr. Sam Vaknin.

About the Author

It is through my life's experiences and through my human connection that I have learned who I am, how to love, and how to give. My very important goal is to teach others to be a better partner in their primary love relationship. Through my experiences I have learned that our communication skills are the key to any successful relationship. Some couples disagree over personality traits or basic gender differences. I want to help everyone understand these differences so you can diffuse those negative feelings. Most relationships end due to misunderstandings and the buildup of anger and resentment. Although my point of view is unconcealed and matter of fact, I simply want to bring the reality of these Bags to light and aid all in love, life, and living.

Quinton Morgan

www.ingramcontent.com/pod-product-compliance
Lightning Source LLC
Chambersburg PA
CBHW072038060426
42449CB00010BA/2324